WRITE LIKE A REBEL

Break the blank page.

ELISE KRENTZEL

Table of Contents

Welcome to Write Like a Rebel!

Are you ready? I want to welcome you personally to the bold journey of writing your non-fiction book, novel, memoir, or instructional how-to manual. You've taken a courageous step to reach this point, and I am stoked to be part of your self-discovery through writing.

I'd love to share a little about myself before we drill down into the nuts and bolts of this course. I've been writing for decades; features, blogs, interviews, travel, science-fiction books, fiction, journals, video scripts, and more, but I haven't published my books until recently. I began writing as a preteen to avoid the crazy household I grew up in. By 17 and still, in H.S., I became a published journalist in a national music magazine in the U.S.A. By 19, I toured with the rock band Kiss in Japan on a press junket that changed my life forever. During the onset of Covid, I sat down and wrote *Under My Skin - Drama, Trauma, & Rock 'n' Roll* about that time in my life: **elisekrentzel.com/books**

Yet in between, I've had several careers and often let writing go, as in 'not doing it.' I promoted punk and alternative rock in Japan, produces videos, did fashion licensing publicity, published digital travel guides, and public relations for non-profits, film festivals, and the arts. Eventually, I found my way back to my first abiding love of WRITING.

Since the pandemic outbreak, I've been coaching others to write their hearts out using the lessons I learned as a self-published author, developmental editor, and all-around publishing junkie.

So now back to you

I designed this course for the writer who has yet to leap by fulfilling the goal of writing their book. At the end of this course you will have completed an outline of a manuscript ready to be edited. With diligence, you *can* complete a first draft. BUT, it is up to you to work the hours to learn and complete the homework assignments in this course.

If this is your first book, I welcome you to the

creative writing world. Even if this is a second or third attempt to finish something you thought about or started long ago, this course will jumpstart and tweak your process without any interference or procrastination to get you on the right track.

What to Expect in Write Like a Rebel

This course consists of written assignments and videos. The videos are accessible by scanning the QR-code code at the beginning of the lessons.

Please take a minute to review the outline presented on the following pages.

Week One: Create the Concept

In Week One, you will create a concept for your original intellectual property work: your book. You will write a 450-word synopsis of what you want the book to be about. You will write the overview including the following elements, and you can use a bullet point format to make changes easier later. The 'arc' is what people in book terminology call the concept.

- Main plot
- Main character(s)
- Main theme

1 video
5 hours to complete

Week Two: Create Your Character Profiles

During Week Two, you'll create character profiles and describe their traits.

1 video
5-7 hours to complete

Week Three: Add Depth to Your Character Profiles

In Week Three, you will use the five senses to describe the characters' personality traits more deeply than in Week Two. This is where you get to shape their persona so they become lifelike.

1 video
4 hours to complete

Week Four: Map Out the Major Events in Your Protagonist's Life

In Week Four, you will list the significant events that impacted and affected the main character's life powerfully. Write the events out on a spreadsheet chronologically. These events shape the background story and develop tension.

6+ hours to complete

Week Five: Map Out the Major Events in the Remaining Character's Lives

In Week Five, you will apply the same techniques learned in Week Four to the other characters in your book.

10+ hours to complete

Week Six: Choose the Tense of Your Story

Determine the tense you will use to write your novel. Test the tense by writing a little. Read about the plot and characters.

3+ hours to complete

Week Seven: Map Out Your Chapters

In Week Seven, get ready to map out and outline your chapters. This is where the plot, characters, events, and themes come together. Write the arc for Chapter One using Week One as a reference.

1 video
5+ hours to complete

Week Eight: Give Titles to Your Chapters

In Week Eight, it's time to get creative and write out the Chapter Titles for as many as possible based on the synopsis (arc) you wrote in Week One.

1 video
6+ hours to complete

Week Nine: How to Compose Dialogue

  In Week Nine, you will learn about dialogue and how to write like a compelling storyteller.

1 video
6+ hours to complete

Week Ten: How to Conduct an Interview

  In Week Ten, you will learn how to interview to gather background research on a person and how to transcribe them into an engaging discussion.

1 video
6 - 12 hours to complete

Week Eleven: Finish the Arc and Outline for All Remaining Chapters

  In Week Eleven, you will reapply the rules of creating an arc - (beginning, middle, and end) for every chapter starting with Chapter Two.

6 - 12 hours to complete

Week Twelve: The Writing Begins

In Week Twelve, your last course session, it's your time to pump up inspiration and focus on finishing up your book. From this point forward, you will continue writing to complete the entire first draft of your manuscript.

1 Video
6-9 hours to complete

Week One

Create the Concept

Watch this week's video

This week, you will create a concept for your original intellectual property work: your book. You will write a 450-750 word synopsis of what you want the book to be about.

The elements of the synopsis can be written in bullet point format to make changes easier later.The concept is known as the 'arc' in book lingo.

- Main plot
- Main character(s)
- Main theme

Whatever your story is now, it will change when you finish writing your first draft. This exercise aims to define the plot (or arc, as we say in the business). Describing the arc as a first step will save you days, if not weeks, of scrambling around trying to make sense of scribblings in notebooks or little fragments of stories you may have begun. The arc is the essence of your story. It is the main plot and defines the over-arching emotional texture of your book.

To get an idea of your first assignment, look at the back cover blurbs of similar books. Let's say you are writing a fictionalized version of actual events, and the book category is a mystery. Start reading what other authors have written. Look at Agatha Christie or Elmore Leonard's back covers to read how they describe their books. Go on Amazon or into a brick-and-mortar bookstore.

The synopsis is usually between 450 - 750 words and should include these elements. You may have to write it several times and edit it until you reach the goal of at most 750 words.

The main plot

Tell the reader the story without going into too much detail. You want people to savor the menu, not chow down an entire meal in a few bites.

Imagine telling someone about your book. That someone has less than two minutes to hear about it. Practice speaking about your plot (arc) before you set it to paper. This helps to get you out of your head and into your heart. Here's a snippet from Al Franken's book blurb, *The Truth, with Jokes*.

> "...If you were a Bush voter, Al wants to set aside partisan bitterness and talk about the better future Americans can build for their children, grandchildren, and great-grandchildren. But first, Al must show you how Republican leaders are, at this very moment, betraying your trust and quite possibly lighting a Cuban cigar with a burning American flag or Bible."

Franken's story's main plot is: getting out the truth behind the lies perpetrated by the Republican party, which is out to destroy American democracy by uncovering their strategies, conversations, and plots.

The main characters

Weave into your plot the main character or characters. There could be multiple characters, and in a memoir, you might be the lead, with family, friends, teachers, and others as supporting characters.

You only need to take broad brushstrokes here without writing details about these characters. Using Al Franken's book *The Truth with Jokes* example, the main character is the author who has done investigative work as a politician sitting in on the meetings he reveals in his non-fiction book. The secondary stream of characters includes former President Bush Jr., and Tom DeLay, although Bush is also the main protagonist in this book.

Adding to the synopsis, the character (in this case, Bush, looks like this).

Al reveals the disturbing story of how Bush (barely) beat Kerry with his campaign of "fear, smear, and queers" and then claimed a nonexistent mandate.

Let's add the first part of the blurb, the plot, and the second part, the characters; this is what we get.

> "...Al wants to bridge partisan divides and discuss a brighter future for all Americans, including future generations, if you voted for Bush. But first, Al must show you how Republican leaders are, at this very moment, betraying your trust and quite possibly lighting a Cuban cigar with a burning American flag or Bible."

Al reveals the disturbing story of how Bush (barely) beat Kerry with his campaign of "fear, smear, and queers" and then claimed a nonexistent mandate."

The central theme

Sometimes the theme is close to the plot, and if you search and dig deep, you will see there is usually more than one theme to a story. If you have a central theme with sub-themes, write them out.

For example, I provided developmental editing and book coaching for one client to get their book into shape from the voluminous notes they offered. The title I created was also the theme: *Management by Intent - The Five Principles*: intentional management. Based on the book, the sub-themes are the five principles on creating deliberate management techniques.

Back to Al Franken's book. The theme of his book is exposing corrupt politicians and their practices. The sub-themes include various campaigns and persons who corroborate the corruption by acting with ill intent, such as Bush Jr., Terri Schiavo, and Tom DeLay.

Finally, let's add the first part of the blurb, the plot, the second part, the characters, and the third part, the theme; this is what we get.

> "...If you were a Bush voter, Al wants to set aside partisan bitterness and talk about the better future Americans can build for their children, grandchildren, and successful-grandchildren. But first, Al must show you how Republican leaders are, at this very moment, betraying your trust and quite possibly lighting a Cuban cigar with a burning American flag or Bible.

Al reveals the disturbing story of how Bush (barely) beat Kerry with his campaign of "fear, smear, and queers." He then claimed a nonexistent mandate." Conservatives sought to undermine Social Security using a strategy borrowed from Vladimir Lenin. Republicans decided that Terri Schiavo will make a "successful political issue."

This synopsis is less than 250 words because I omitted a few paragraphs from the sleeve.

Think of the summary as a thesis statement. Do not summarize initially. You'll have ample time to edit your synopsis after you've jumped through a few hoops.

I knew the story's theme and arc for my book before I sat down to write it. The motivation and feelings behind the theme are what your synopsis entails. Read about *Under My Skin - Drama, Trauma & Rock n Roll* here: elisekrentzel.com/books

Here's a short snippet from the back cover of another book.

> "In this right-moving memoir, a young man saves a baby magpie as his estranged father is dying only to find that caring for the mischievous bird has saved him."

If you are a businessperson, consider the synopsis a mission statement.

Laying the foundation for writing a book is essential in creating a compelling and engaging story. This process involves careful planning while considering factors such as the book's goals, readers, format, and necessary research.

Pro Tip

One of the first steps in laying the foundation for writing a book is to define the purpose and goals of the book. It involves identifying what message or story the book aims to convey, the intended audience, and the desired outcomes. For example, a memoir may seek to share a personal journey of growth and self-discovery with readers. A business book may aim to provide practical insights and advice for professionals in a particular industry. By clearly defining the purpose and goals of the book, you, the author, can ensure that the writing process stays on track and that the final product meets the intended objectives.

Homework:

Write your synopsis!

NOTES

NOTES

Week Two

Create Your
Character Profiles

Watch this week's video

This week, you will create profiles for your major characters and outline all their traits.

Start by listing the characters who will be part of your story. Obviously, if your book is a memoir or fictionalized biography, you will begin with yourself as the main protagonist.

Add character names in a spreadsheet or document.

Then begin to list their traits. Think of this exercise as building an avatar for each person, including but not limited to the following. Start with the obvious.

Physical traits

- Height
- Weight
- Body shape
- Hair - color, length, and style
- Eyes - color, shape, size of lashes, eyebrow shape
- Mouth - shape, measurement of lips, distance to chin and nose
- Gait - how do they walk, racewalking fast, hard, slow, dragging their heels, limping
- Twitches - where on the body, what type of twitch?
- Holding the space -
  - How they hold their hands when they speak
  - How they use their hands when angry or happy.
  - How they use their arms to express themselves

- Describe the attributes identifying a character, such as glasses, hats, and earrings.

Now, you'll need to dig a little more into the mindset of each of the characters. How do they decide? Are they driven by emotion or logic? Are they educated, and how? There are five different thinkers with their thinking styles: synthesists, idealists, pragmatists, analysts, and realists. Start with these examples below and fill in the rest.

Mental traits

- Synthesists stand out with their creativity and curiosity; they consider different ideas, views, and possibilities.
- Idealists are constantly setting and working toward big goals—they set the bar high and expect others to do the same.
- Pragmatists take a logical approach to problem-solving; they focus on immediate results instead of long-term effects.
- Analysts are interested in the facts and data points—they have a straightforward procedure for doing everything.
- Realists are the perfect problem-solvers; they tackle problems head-on and don't feel challenged by your everyday conundrums.

By the end of this session, you will have a lovely portrait of each character physically, mentally, and visually.

Homework

Create the profiles for each character and bullet point all their traits. Imagine yourself talking to someone about these characters. Keep that in mind when creating them. Have fun!

Pro Tips:

Memory Booster Prompts

- What's something they were afraid of as a child?
- What's something difficult he/she/they had to do or endure?
- What's an embarrassing moment that happened?
- Who is someone he/she/they lost? What are their memories about that person?
- What's something that helped to shape his/her/their outlook on life? (Do this in stages as our view of life changes as we age)
- Describe the teachers at school.
- Describe their best childhood friend and their relationship with this person.

- When they were a child, how did they imagine their adult self?
- What's their earliest memory? Or memories from 0-5 years old?
- What are some of the memories they associate with springtime? With summer, fall, and winter?

Write about the characters first
- Early years at home
- Neighborhood
- Neighbors
- Relatives
- Day of school or college
- Crush
- Date or physical attraction
- Car
- Pet
- Job
- Life milestones
- Death in the family
- Graduation
- Wedding
- Divorce
- Pregnancy

- Childbirth
- Job
- Major career change
- Retirement

Five Senses
- Fragrances
- Pine needles or other natural scents
- Grandparent or another relative
- Cut grass
- Flowers, i.e., roses
- Sunscreen
- Horses or other animals
- Rubbing alcohol
- Mother's cooking, what foods?
- Spices
- Stale beer
- Pencil erasers
- Vinegar
- Newly-vacuumed carpet
- Orange peel
- Knitted sweaters or other clothing
- Radiators heating
- Mothballs
- A new car

- Frying bacon
- Damp paper

Important life milestones and how have they impacted your/her/his/their life?

- Being a parent
- Your parent
- Your grandparent
- A sister or brother
- A sport or game, or competition
- Gardening
- Trip(s) you took
- A particular job
- Your career
- Something you collect(ed)
- An unusual talent
- Dieting or fitness
- Your cultural heritage
- A romance or affair(s)
- Marriage
- Divorce
- S spiritual awakening
- Esp and other invisible realities like deja vu or UFO sighting
- Farming

- Your relationship with nature
- A school you went to
- Your college or university
- Summer camp
- Your house
- A pet
- An illness
- A disability
- An accident
- An addiction
- The death of someone close to you
- Childhood
- Adolescence
- Becoming an adult
- Middle age
- Mature age
- A book or movie that changed your life
- A work of art that changed your life
- A teacher or mentor
- An important friendship
- A spiritual or religious experience
- A change in your economic situation
- A decision to change some aspect of your life
- A place where you lived

- A place that was special to you
- A move to a new place
- Another major life change
- The effect of war on your Life
- Another historical event that impacted your life
- Food
- Chores
- A dangerous situation you survived
- Something you did to help others
- Military service
- Something you accomplished
- A topic you research as a hobby
- The discrimination you have faced
- Someone who was a great inspiration to you
- A mission or quest
- A work of art

NOTES

Watch this week's video

This week, you will use the five senses to describe the characters' personality traits more deeply than in Week Two. This is where you get to shape their persona so they become lifelike.

Until this point, you have mastered what the characters look like, how they move in 3D, and what motivates them to think the way they do. How a person conducts themselves reflects their values. Here's where you get to make a big impression on your reader by how your character lives their life. It's time now in Week Three to add the finishing touches to each character; this is how you'll do it.

Speech

- **Accents**
  - Southern
  - European
  - Asian
  - African
  - Latin American
  - Other

- **Slang**
  - Imma, gonna
  - Urban dictionary slang
  - New York 'cawfee.'
  - Boston 'paak the caar'
  - British – various depending on the region, ie: Manchester, Liverpool, London (east end or west end)
  - Other

- **Enunciation**
  - Less educated
  - Educated overseas, what does it sound like?

- Excellent diction
- Understands the difference between sounds like P, H, T, and D

Smells/Odor

- Do they have a signature perfume?
- What does the perfume or cologne smell like?
- Do they smell old? Describe it
- Is there a lingering odor or scent? Describe it
- Is there a lingering fragrance, such as their grandmother's or mother's cooking, associated with this character?
- Do they smoke cigarettes or weed?

Taste

- What do they eat? What is the frequency with which they eat certain foods?
  - Casual eaters
  - Vegan
  - Vegetarian
  - Omnivore
  - Pescatarian

- Fast-food
- Meat only, no veggies
- Kosher
- Halal
- Gluten-free
- How do they eat?
  - Do they shovel the food into their mouth?
  - Do they masticate slowly?
  - Do they talk with their mouth full with food?
  - Do they take dainty bites?
  - Do they cut their food European style or American style?
  - Do they know how to use a knife and fork?
  - Do they only use a fork?
- What do they drink?
- Drinking?
  - Do they slurp when drinking a bowl of soup?
  - Do they slather all over themself?
  - Do they sip gracefully?
  - Do they hold their teacup from the bottom of the cup with one hand on the cup?

Look & Dress Code

- Dashing
- Debonair
- Punk
- Sloppy/PJ look
- Western
- European
- Scruffy shoes

Describe their clothing in detail. Do they have a signature piece like a brooch or a specific color tie they wear? Do they wear only skirts or pants? What type of pants do they wear - jeans? If so, how are they worn? Tight, loose, Levis straight leg. You catch the drift.

Don't forget that the antagonist of your protagonist must come across just as absolute as the main character. There is a tendency sometimes to plow through the description or take the secondary character(s) for granted just because they don't seem as necessary, but that would be a mistake. We need to understand them as well as the main character.

Have you ever read a book or seen a film where you're left hanging or questioning why you didn't know more about a character or how the story ends for them? That is something to be mindful of, not to let happen.

Once you've finished adding these finishing touches to your characters, you will be ready for Week Four.

Pro Tip

Character & Place Prompts

- What might be unique about the place this character lives in that a person passing through might not notice or understand?

- How does s/he feel when s/he is there?

- What memory or emotion does the place evoke in them and why?

- Can you come up with something that happened there that ties into the wound from their past? Tie it to hope or dream they may have had but lost somewhere.

- How do they look at the place and the life they had there (professional, family, community)?

- What is the one special secret place they like to visit, and what do they do there?

- What is the one place they avoid and would never go to?

- What can they notice while there that no one else sees?

- What happened in this special place that revealed something secret about them? About their dreams? About their fears?

- What one (or more) memories can you come up with that is triggered by them being in this place?

- What was/is their happiest moment in this place?

- What is their saddest moment in this place?

- If they have returned after some time, how has this place changed for them,

- How does the change make them feel? Happy, sad, nostalgic, fearful?

- What conflicting feelings do they have about being there?

Homework

Write about every character's personality traits using the five senses to describe each. I like to use a spreadsheet for easier access to the categories I create. Do what works for you to keep track of your writing.

Week Four

Map Out the Major Events in Your Protagonist's Life

amo
"It thing

This week, detail the key events that influenced your main character. Think of this exercise as if you were the Wizard of Oz, sitting high above the mortal coil, watching and reviewing the life events that you created for your character (whether this protagonist is yourself or someone else; you need an objective lens by which to see them from a distance to home in on the details). What events surrounded and changed their lives or challenged their psychological, physical, emotional, or mental state of being? What circumstances had a lifelong impact on the main character?

Here are two ways to write it

- **First method**.

  Write the events chronologically on a time-line starting at either year zero (feelings of the mother in the womb affect a newborn and could have had lasting repercussions) or at the earliest age you want the character's story to begin with. What happened to the main character? If they directly influence other characters, write the event(s) from the main character's perspective. In Week Five, you will duplicate this exercise for each character who plays a secondary role in your book from the main character's vantage point.

- **Second method**.

  Write out the most harrowing, joyous, or tragic occasion laterally (try using a word art generator such as https://wordart.com. What this free tool does is organize the words by important theme. I've used it for my book, *Under My Skin - Drama, Trauma & Rock 'n' Roll*. Imagine squeezing a lemon. The pits are the events, while the juice is the adjective to describe the event. You must distill each event into one word. In my case, the words included: sex, abortion, Europe, travel, Japan, rock band, touring, leaving (home), and suicide.

Once you have the distilled words, you can freely build the event. Using the example of the word *suicide* from my word art, the event was *swallowing a whole bottle of Joseph Aspirin for Children when I was four years old.* Your timeline could look like this.

E.g., 1964 - Bronx, New York, in the apartment - swallowed a bottle of aspirin. I almost died.

I've added the year, the city, the state (place), and where within that city, state (the apartment) the event occurred.

Some events may overlap and affect more than one character. This is because how a character is impacted is vastly different from one to the other. In the above example, my mother was significantly affected. From my four-year- perspective, I wrote the overlap event in my timeline like this:

E.g., Mom - 1964 - Bronx, New York, rushes Elise to the hospital.

When you get to Week Five and revisit this event, you will write it from the experience of the mother character, and it may look like this.

E.g., Mom - 1964 - Bronx, New York, rushes Elise to the hospital. She faints on the route and almost has a panic attack that requires medical attention.

These events shape the background story and develop tension.

Homework

Use a spreadsheet or Word doc to map out the significant events that affected your main character. Use details to help you develop: year, location, place, interior environment, background music, or external events that had nothing to do with your character.

NOTES

Week Five

Map Out the Major Events in the Remaining Character's Lives

amo
"It thing

This week, as in Week Four, you will list the significant events that affected the remaining characters' lives. It's best to begin Week Five with a list of the remaining characters and call them the supporting cast in order of importance. If you are writing a memoir, you will probably be impacted by your parents, siblings (if you had any), institutions you attended, authority figures from teachers, other adults, friends, or work colleagues. Yet not all of these supporting actors had the same impact.

Write a list using one of the two methods mentioned in Week Four, from the most important characters to the minor yet essential characters in the plot. Use bullet points to create a list of the events that shaped each person's life. Again, remember to focus on what changed, challenged, or had a lifelong psychological, physical, emotional, or mental impact on these people.

Whether you are writing fiction or non-fiction, the events and characters need to be authentic, believable, and honest to themselves. Even when their "honesty" means their behavior is incongruous and they're lying, cheating, stealing, addicted, or what have you.

Homework

As you made a spreadsheet or Word doc last week, you will map out all the significant events that affected your secondary and supporting characters in Week Five. The events may overlap with your main character; however, the difference is that when you bullet point each of these characters' circumstances, it will be from their point of view.

NOTES

NOTES

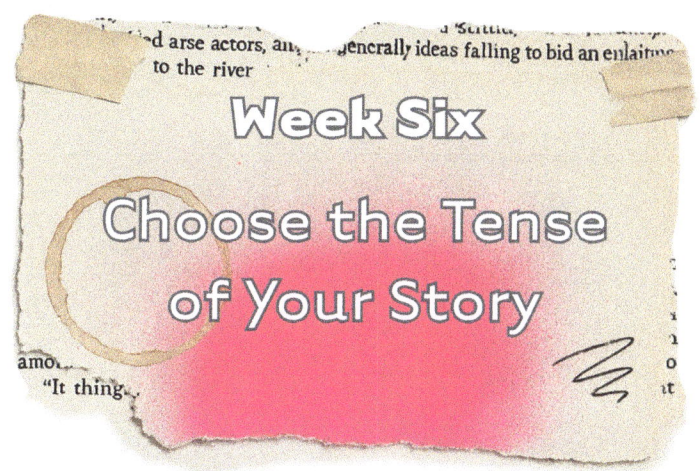

Week Six

Choose the Tense of Your Story

This week, you'll determine in which tense you will write your novel. Decide whether you will write your book in the first-person, second-, or third-person narrative. How do you choose, though?

- The 1st person's POV (point-of-view) uses the pronouns I, We, Me, My, Us, Our, Myself, and Ourselves.

- The 2nd person POV uses the pronoun you, your, and third-person POV words like hers, they, and itself, but not "I" or "us."

- The 3rd person's POV uses the pronouns "she," "he," "they," and "it."

- The 3rd person is limited when the narrator only knows and writes about one person's thoughts.

- The 3rd person omniscient is when the narrator knows the thoughts of more than just one person.

You can mix 1st person and 3rd person limited or omniscient. There are no rules against it. If your book is a character-driven story, write it in the first person. But the choice is yours and what feels natural to you. I come from a journalistic background and tend to "report." Writing in the first person makes it easy.

Character-driven means what it sounds like; the character's makeup, personality, thoughts, feelings, inner life, soul, and spirit are entwined in the telling. There is rarely a separation between the aspects of the total human experience. Of course, some characters act in silos, think in categories, and shut out the connection with a greater force. Even those characters may be hiding their inner nature or inner demons from themselves and, therefore, cannot detach from the fact that, as human beings, we are whole.

Fantasy author Beth Alvarez has this to say about character-driven stories, "If you're looking for a character-driven story, a good example is *Game of Thrones*. The story in *Game of Thrones* happens because of complicated actions and interactions occurring between characters. Every time someone decides, it radically alters the story's path. And if we removed these interactions, there wouldn't be much plot left.

Study Reading of Excellent Character-Driven Novels

- *The Old Man and the Sea*, Ernest Hemingway
- *To Kill a Mockingbird*, Harper Lee
- *The Joy Luck Club*, Amy Tan
- *The Catcher in the Rye*, J.D Salinger

Plot-driven stories are primarily about external events that lead characters into bizarre situations, places, or thought processes to take specific actions. Murakami's *1Q84* is plot-driven and follows two protagonists, Tengo and Aomame, entering an alternate universe set in the year *1Q84*. The characters and their development are essential to the story, but external events and changes drive it. Having read everything he's written, I categorize his books as magic realism or fantasy. I lean more toward science fiction and dystopian than fantasy.

Study Reading of Excellent Plot-Driven Novels

- *1Q84,* Haruki Murakami
- *The Glass Castle*, Jeannette Walls
- *In Cold Blood*, Truman Capote
- *Midnight in the Garden of Good and Evil*, John Berendt

You may not have time to read all the books mentioned, so please choose one from the lists based on if you are writing a character or plot-based novel. Follow this guide and consider the genre you are writing.

- In nonfiction, authors commonly use the second person POV, but they also employ the first person for memoirs.
- Mystery/Thriller/Suspense: Third-person limited
- Children's/Middle grade: limited, although Omniscient is familiar with narrators like The Hobbit.

If you're unsure how to choose a perspective, here's an assignment to assist you.

Homework

Write a few lines from each perspective mentioned: first, second, or third person. Try a couple of paragraphs for each viewpoint. If you already know which voice you'd like to use at this juncture, great! If not, it's best to decide clearly which perspective you will use because the writing will commence in a few more weeks. You want to be fully prepared before the creative process begins.

I liken the process to building a house. An architect must lay the foundation in blueprint form before the builders can dig around to pour concrete into the ground. This also applies to writing a book. 😊

NOTES

Week Seven

Map Out Your Chapters

Watch this week's video

This week, you'll map out and outline your chapters based on the information you've compiled thus far. Summarizing each chapter's beginning, middle, and end will aid you to complete the arc for every chapter. You will apply the same methods to outline each chapter as you wrote a synopsis during Week One. You are halfway through the course, and it's a big turning point for you and your writing. The plot, characters, events, and themes come together during Week Seven.

Look at the example below of the outline of chapter one and arc from one of my client's books, You've *Got to Lose to Win,* by Will Simpson.

Sample of the Outline for *You've Got to Lose to Win* (Chapter 1)

Rick and Slade (the main characters) physically build a poker table in the living room of Slade's new duplex. Once finished, they set up the room and prepared the food for Slade's first hosted poker game that evening. Slade is proud and ready to make a good impression, but things don't go as planned.

The Arc

- Beginning – Setting up the room with Rick
- Middle - Problem – Bill bails out (another important secondary character), and the entire game is in jeopardy. One-third of the players have bailed right before the game begins - the game is all but dead, and Rick and Slade scramble to get players lined up to play.
- End - The players are replaced, and the game is back on.

Knowing the genre of this book, fiction (based on facts and people), I worked with the author to build a framework for his story chapter by chapter. You are questioning the reasons why certain characters acted the way they did, allowing for a wide berth of variable outcomes. In chapter one, the game was almost forfeited by Bill's actions. Ultimately, the game went on due to Slade's clear foresight and plan B, which Rick had no clue about.

Homework

Write the outline using the arc method for your first Chapter using Week One as a reference. If you've already outlined (in your mind) the chapters, begin on the arc for other chapters. There is no rush to do this; some people are urged to complete tasks linearly. If you'd like to take a shot at writing out the arcs for more chapters than just the first one, this is up to you.

Pro Tip

If you are on a creative "roll," don't stop unless you have demanding chores like feeding your baby, taking care of an elderly relative, or even going to work (how novel is that? 😃), you may have to discontinue even if you don't want to stop. Follow your gut and keep writing until ready to hit the hay. Take advantage of the incredible burst of energy found when you are on a proverbial "roll."

NOTES

NOTES

Week Eight

Give Title to Your Chapters

Watch this week's video

This week, you will get creative. Go back to the synopsis you wrote in Week One and make sure that it stands up and is what you want for the book. Based on the synopsis, write the Chapter Titles for as many chapters as possible.

Don't worry; it's not as daunting as it seems. Words are more accessible when you are relaxed and sometimes when you aren't even thinking about the subject. If you recall, during last week's session (Week Seven), you reviewed a chapter outline from a book one of my clients wrote. Once he outlined the chapters, we revisited them to determine the best titles.

Let's look at the title he chose for his first chapter.

Chapter One from *You've Got to Lose to Win* was given the title "Shuffle Up and Deal?"

The question mark was added to provide tension since the main character Slade needed to learn how the evening would turn out once Bill pulled out of the game. Would anyone else show up? Are enough players for a poker game? At the eleventh hour, other players did show up, and the game was back on again. Yet the reader would find that out at the very end of chapter one. This title is a teaser, intrigues the reader, and is true to the crux of the chapter.

All titles are fluid, meaning you needn't get hung up on just one. Develop one or several because you can change them later on. Refining and editing afterward are my working modus operandi.

To hook the reader, the beginning of a chapter needs to have an element of edginess, mystery, explosiveness, curiosity, and some emotional highs and lows. It can be reflective or funny. Reel the reader in. Determine the tone and theme of the chapter and base it on the location, geography, personalities, and events that occur throughout the chapter. All these parts will give you the oomph and ammunition needed to create an excellent catchy title.

In my first book *Under My Skin - Drama, Trauma & Rock 'n' Roll,* the titles intrigued enough readers online, and at book signings to buy the book without reading the back blurb (synopsis)! I was amused to see people react as they scrolled through the table of contents. Their eyebrows lifted, and they smiled or chuckled. Chapter Six is entitled *Fucking My Way Through Europe.* You can imagine what happens in that chapter just from the title, no? The chapter titles, like mine, can be explicit or open-ended, like Will Simpson's in *Shuffle Up and Deal?*

There is no right or wrong way to title each chapter. The title is unique to your book and no one else's.

Homework

Since you've outlined the chapter(s) in Week Seven, write out potential chapter titles for as many as you want. This homework will be great fun.

Pro Tips

When speaking with someone about a writing project I'm working on, I take my iPhone and record the conversation with their permission. 🙂Sometimes, I surprise myself with the incredible morsels unconsciously pouring out of my mouth. Had I not recorded the conversation, I then wish I had.

Another tip is to go outside in the woods or nature and bring a notebook and a writing instrument. I do not advocate the use of an electronic device. Using a pen - slower than a keyboard - allows me to hone in on my undeveloped thoughts. Let's call it the slow writing movement. The pen allows me to daydream and catch up with the words when I'm ready to write.

The third tip is to look at the episode titles from one of your favorite TV series. Choose one episode and analyze it. Break it into the beginning, middle, and ending, and map out the main plot, theme, and events. Then go back to your chapter(s) and do the same.

NOTES

NOTES

Week Nine

How to Compose Dialogue

Watch this week's video

This week, you will learn how to compose dialogue. Writing an engaging conversation that keeps the reader on the edge of their seat is a skill, and writing great dialogue is a talent that takes practice and nurturing. Refresh your memory by flipping through some of your favorite books, and rereading a few pages to see how the author wrote the dialogue.

Some books written in the first person have little back-and-forth between characters. In contrast, others, like *Tokyo Vice - An American Reporter on the Police Beat in Japan* by Jake Adelstein, are driven by dialogue. That makes sense since the main character, Jake, *is* a reporter. Here are a few lines of dialogue from his book.

"...I tried to make conversation with some folks who were hanging around the edges of the police barrier, looking up at the building...I found a foreman who had a picture of her - snack-mama was surprisingly heavy."

"Do you have any idea who would want to kill her?" I asked, deep in reporter mode.

"Hmmm, I don't know. Maybe some deadbeat customer who ran up a huge tab. She could really ride your ass if you didn't pay your bill on time. I've known loan sharks who were more easy-going."

This wasn't precisely a quotable comment about the deceased. "What about her husband?" I asked.

"Not around. She lived with her daughter. People said they weren't getting along. Something about the daughter's boyfriend."

"Was he a yakuza or just some kind of badass?"

"Nope. Worse. He was a foreigner."

In this conversation, it's easy to follow who is speaking. The author doesn't need to state the person's name after each sentence. Specifically, Jake (the reporter) was talking to a person at the crime scene. It's clear who is leading the questioning and answering.

The point of good dialogue is to make it relevant to the story. No one needs to read boring conversations such as below unless they are relevant to the story. Dialogue needs to exemplify the thoughts of the character.

"Oh yeah; he said it was fine."

"Right, I'll be over in thirty minutes."

"Text me tomorrow about the date."

You see this type of dialogue in films. You can imagine a conversation in a film by examining the expressions on the faces of the speakers. On the page, it's another animal. As an author, you must create the images and drop in hints through verbal clues for the reader to follow. Dialogue **IS** simply conversation. But that doesn't mean you'll add every sound, sigh, or filler words such as overused Americanisms "like," "um," or "you know."

Pro Tips

Write as your characters speak. Whether recreating them based on real characters or molding them from scratch, you're writing in their voice. A magical occurrence happens once you're writing. The characters take over your mind and speak for themselves. When this happens to you, allow them to voice their thoughts and act as a vessel for expression. You're not crazy, so don't think you are! You are in the zone.

No matter how much time you've allocated for the assignment, chuck that clock, and be present to your character's voice. A fascinating process emerges where you grow with the character. It's akin to an actor who takes on a role, and once s/he/they memorize the lines, they begin to embody the character. That is the litmus test of good writing. Refer to the previous work you completed in Weeks Three and Four.

NOTES

d arse actors, an... ...enerally ideas falling to bid an enlai...
to the river

Week Ten

How to Conduct an Interview

amo...
"It thing...

Watch this week's video

This week, you will learn how to interview, transcribe and write them. You may be writing a story that requires you, the author, to research, meet people and interview them as subjects for a non-fiction biography or memoir. If the bio is multi-generational or an epic tale, the key to mastering the interview process will aid you by providing positive feedback from the subjects.

If one of your characters is a journalist, TV anchor, or news reporter, learning the process and best practices of how the interviewing game works gives you a leg up in credibility. The most famous writers, like Stephen King or Margaret Atwood, research their subjects, careers and become semi-experts. Writing credibly about a topic enables you to extract the necessary information. Willing participants shed their secrets by confiding in you. Look at the late great TV host of *60 Minutes* (among many other accomplishments in her career), Barbara Walters! She was able to get heads of state to share intimacies with her.

I started my writing career as a journalist who, by default, interviewed rock bands, celebrities, and the people behind the scenes in the music and electronic industries. How did I learn that? Well, in part, I had an innate talent. As a child, I was a curious observer of people's behavior, and that hasn't changed to this day. I wanted to get to the root of who they were, what made them tick, and why they behaved in the manner they did. I'd ask many questions, which my mother was embarrassed about as they were direct and pointed. That's how children are, without filters! I've kept up the practice of a bare filter when interacting with others during an interview. Being a direct straight arrow has benefits, mainly throwing people off guard. Before you dig deeper to find out how and why they felt intimate, **ALWAYS** begin the interview with a statement to set the tone.

Scenario

Amy Boeckerstette is other abled. She has Downs Syndrome; others with a similar condition might find it challenging to function in a competitive environment like golf. Amy was the first other abled person to play golf professionally and win. She inspired more than a million others worldwide on YouTube. https://youtu.be/iayUXiu_bqY

Statement

Amy, your self-confidence is an inspiration to millions of people. We understand that no person is an island, and the encouragement of loved ones makes taking risks seem easier.

Wait for the reaction and *then* launch into the questions. Here are a few I used when interviewing Amy Boeckerstette.

1. Who is the most influential person that supported you in your life?
2. How did they show their support?
3. How would you like your success to influence others needing more confidence?
4. What advice would you give to someone with Down's who wants to play golf?
5. Describe when you were at your lowest point

and how this person got you out of your comfort zone.

This last question was more poignant and profound than the previous four icebreakers. Those questions did not put Amy off in the slightest. Yet if she were, then you could follow with questions that question her reaction, such as

1. "Tell me why this question took you off guard?"
2. "Did this offend you? If so, explain why?
3. What happened to you earlier in life to cause your reaction?"
4. "Are you thinking of someone else now?"

When interviewing live, whether via Zoom or in-person, record the session unless you are a super stenographer. You can also take notes to remind yourself of critical questions and answers. I do both, which best covers my bases in case I forget something crucial. Once you're ready to transcribe the notes, you'll need twice as long to type out the notes as it took to conduct the interview. Be prepared.

If you are writing an epic tale, family history, biography, or memoir, consider investing in an AI transcription tool such as Plaud, or if you have an iPhone you can simply use VoiceMemos to record, transcribe and download the raw transcription.

Pro Tips

- Know your subject by researching their life.
- Consider interviewing significant others of the subject before the interview for background information, impressions, and examples of their interactions with the subject.
- During the interview, be provocative; otherwise, your questions may appear superficial.
- Allow spontaneity. Your interview subject may stray from your script or discuss a topic you missed during your research. See where it goes, and allow it to flow.
- If you're on the clock and time is limited, facilitate the subject by interjecting your question, in case they are waxing prolific.
- Show emotion and interest while questioning your subject. Gesticulate, smile and show surprise. Nothing says, 'I'm listening to you,' then the questions you ask someone about their life.

NOTES

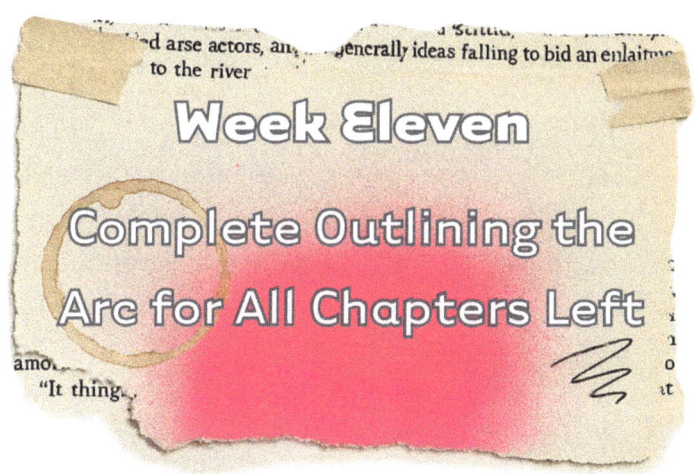

Week Eleven

Complete Outlining the Arc for All Chapters Left

Pat yourself on the back! You are almost at the finish line in this course. You've completed your first draft of Chapter One. Yay! Perhaps you've done more? If you have, then double bravo to you. 😄

Wherever you are right now, you'll need to complete the process of writing the arc and outlines for the remaining chapters.

You will want to take your time with this, as it's not meant to be written all at once, or even over a week. Spread it out if you wish. Some people benefit from deadlines, and others feel restricted by them.

Once you're done with the arc and outline of the book, and then go out and celebrate. You've achieved the next milestone in the writing process. From here on, give yourself another month or two but not longer, to complete the first draft of your book.

Writing is like software development, in a manner of speaking. It takes iterations upon iterations to get it right. But then, at some point, you just have to, one day, throw down the gauntlet and agree to stop developing, stop editing, proofreading, and accept the finished product.

Review the Characters

After you've finished the draft of your manuscript, review the characters as if you are meeting them for the first time. If you have written a business, how-to, or management guideline book, there will most likely be no other main character besides yourself, the teacher. If people do appear in such a book, they will most likely will be clients' and their case studies

In either of these cases, you want to make sure **the reader** knows the answers to the following questions.

- Is there anything they would find confusing? A good method of discovering the answer to this question is to read it aloud to someone close who will be brutally honest with you.

- Are there any pointers, tips, or recommendations they wouldn't understand?
- Are there any moral, psychological, behavioral, or philosophical lessons? If yes, are they clearly understood?
- What questions do they ask you?

NOTES

NOTES

Week Twelve
The Writing Begins

Watch this week's video

Ta-da! Congratulations, you've made it to the end of the course. For Week Twelve, you have the tools to finish writing the rest of the book. You've laid the foundation:

- The summary of your book,
- The arc of the book
- The angle of Chapter One
- The outline of Chapter One
- The title of Chapter One

Nothing can stop you now. Before you begin writing, try this technique.

Exercise to Get Your Mojo Going

This exercise will get your creative juices flowing. Prepare your desk. Do you like coffee or tea or another beverage? Do you close your blinds or open the shades? Do you prefer quiet or music? Shut your door to the room and put up a *Do Not Disturb* handmade sign if you have school-aged children that can read.

Prepare your desktop with tabs or a notebook open to the page with Chapter One's arc and title. Or C+P to a new document for this chapter.

Put a timer on and then:

Close your eyes. Imagine your chapter is done, and you're reading it aloud to a friend or family member for the first time. You feel accomplished and want to kick up your heels in celebration. The feeling overtakes you. In that blissful moment, open your eyes and begin writing. If you feel stuck at any point or have the urge to edit, STOP! Your first draft is just that, a draft. Editing while writing ruins the process and keeps you in your head. Of course, writing is cerebral in the same way reading music is. However, the composition must come from your gut, intuition, or heart to be convincing, authentically you, and original. If you find yourself speaking negatively to yourself, like "I made so many mistakes," "I can't do this," or excusing yourself, "I'm so busy," or "This is too hard or takes too much time," then STOP! Clear those thoughts, and try again. And again.

James Joyce

James Joyce was an Irish writer and poet known for his avant-garde modernism and somewhat hard-to-digest greatest epic, Ulysses. Here's his advice.

Don't Read Literature

'I have not read a work of literature for several years. My head is full of pebbles, rubbish, broken matches, and bits of glass picked up 'most everywhere.' – Letter From Museum Collection.

Literature is writing that gets talked about in universities and lecture halls. But literature can be dangerous, too: if you are stuck to the classics, you miss all the new stuff.

In summary, Joyce advocated for writers to write well rather than aim to write literature.

Pro Tips

During the writing process, here's a reminder to catch yourself and STOP if you find you are:

- Editing sentences as you write
- Using a spellchecker to correct typos
- Proofreading each line as you're typing it
- Allowing distractions and interruptions to hamper your progress, such as phone calls, emails, social media pings, or people
- You are itching to read an unfinished bit aloud to a friend or loved one. Wait until you've finished writing a chapter or a few chapters to prevent outside influences at such an early stage.

Finish the Remaining Chapters

Since you've worked to the end of the course, you now have the wherewithal to write the rest of your manuscript. And you will! Remember to ask yourself some questions in between chapters. Does this story sound interesting to me? If it does, keep on your path. If your answer is negative, analyze why and make the appropriate changes.

Read the Entire Manuscript Aloud

The cadence of your book needs to be like a musical composition, a symphony. The way to discover if it is in harmony is to read it aloud. There are two very different processes in your brain, one if you read it to yourself and the other when you read it aloud.

I've caught more errors in my manuscript when I read it to friends than when reviewing it silently. You will inevitably see the disqualifiers when you can hear yourself read it.

A 250-page book may take half a day to read aloud, and I recommend you hunker down on the weekend and do it in one go. If you find yourself stopping, make a note then and there for future reference. If the listener asks a question or doesn't understand a passage, ask for clarification and, again, take some notes.

Once you're done writing, if you'd like to book coaching sessions with me, please go to calendly.com/ekrentzel. Writing your book is the first step in the process of getting your book to market. Even if you have a publishing deal with a traditional publisher (which is not always the best option for unknown authors), you must edit and publish your book.

If you plan on self-publishing, you will certainly be the one to produce your book. At EK Editorial & Coaching we offer editing and pre-publishing. Check out our services at **elisekrentzel.com/services**. By buying this book, you will automatically get a 25% discount off any of the services offered.

Thank you for participating in Write Like a Rebel. Go get em' Rebels!

Xo
Elise Krentzel

NOTES

About Elise Krentzel

Elise Krentzel was born with a flair for words. As a pre-teen, she discovered her writing talent, starting with diaries and poetry, and while in high school, she was published as a music journalist. Her big break came in 1977, touring Japan with KISS before becoming the Tokyo Bureau Chief of Billboard Magazine.

With a career spanning media, communications, and digital publishing, she's never put down the pen—or her curiosity. Think of her as an archeologist for your ideas, unearthing the hidden gems buried in your mind. Through ghostwriting, personalized coaching, publishing services, and online courses, she shapes your treasures into powerful, polished stories. As a storyteller, she finds endless joy in painting vivid canvases for her books and yours.

A world traveler who has lived in 5 countries on 3 continents, Elise currently calls Austin, Texas home unless she is nomading elsewhere. She is the proud mother of one son.

"Writing isn't just my passion it's the spark that fuels my purpose."